RUN SALMON RUN

Written by
Robyn Hardy & Lorraine Pond

Illustrated by
Lori Joy Smith

A
Bobs & LoLo
BOOK

Published by: Bobolo Productions Inc.
Text copyright © 2014 Bobolo Productions Inc.
Illustration copyright © 2014 Lori Joy Smith

1st printing, 2014

ISBN: 978-0-9938224-0-7

This book is typeset in Gill Sans and Cronos Pro.
Design: Mario Vaira

Printed in Canada
Manufactured by Friesens in Altona, Manitoba, Canada

Supported by the Province of British Columbia

This project is supported by the BC Government's Buy Local Program; delivered by the Investment Agriculture Foundation of BC with funding from the BC Ministry of Agriculture.

Disclaimer: The BC Ministry of Agriculture is committed to working with industry partners. Opinions expressed in this document are those of Robyn Hardy & Lorraine Pond and not necessarily those of the BC Ministry of Agriculture or the Investment Agriculture Foundation.

Acknowledgements

This special book has existed in our hearts for more than a decade. Since we first began writing stories through our music, we have dreamed about giving life to our words on the printed page. Our sincere gratitude is offered to the BC Salmon Marketing Council for entrusting us with the creative leadership on this project. We also extend our warmest thanks to Ursula Vaira at Leaf Press for her guidance, editorial wisdom and encouragement. In addition, we send our heartfelt appreciation to the creative team behind this book. Our thanks to Lori Joy Smith for sharing her incredible talents and bringing her signature splash of colour and fun to these pages. For the design and layout, alongside endless hours of creative consultation, writing revisions and late night review sessions, we give our utmost appreciation to Mario Vaira. We close with one wish that children, families, caregivers and educators alike will share this story together and celebrate wild salmon and the amazing world we are all connected to for generations to come.

Best fishes!

Bobs & LoLo

This story begins
unlike any other.

It starts
at the end
for a father
and mother.

They finish their
journey with
one final wish...

...that the story
continues through
new baby fish.

Run salmon run, beneath the moon and sun. The salmon story circles. Run salmon run.

Tiny round egg
in a gravel nest,
thousands all around
each one like the rest.

Tiny round egg
you grow on your own,
hidden below in a
freshwater home.

Grow egg grow, as the currents flow. The salmon story circles. Grow egg grow.

Little alevin you have just hatched.
No longer an egg, yolk sac still attached.
Little alevin, wiggle in the dark.
The great ocean calls, "Leave the nest! Make your mark!"

Wiggle alevin wiggle, in the shadow of the eagle.
The salmon story circles. Wiggle alevin wiggle.

Small hungry fry, peek from the gravel.
Leaving the shadows to start on your travels.
Small hungry fry, drift in the stream.
The swift current whispers,
          "Go on. Live your dream!"

Drift fry drift, in the stream sure and swift. The salmon story circles. Drift fry drift.

Young little fry, bigger every day.
Quicker and stronger, finding your way.
Young little fry, learn scents that are near.
It may be years before you return here.

Learn fry learn. The river bends and turns. The salmon story circles. Learn fry learn.

Bold silver smolt,
swim in a school.
Go to the ocean with
all your new tools.

Bold silver smolt,
you dart and you race.

You have arrived.
Explore this wild place!

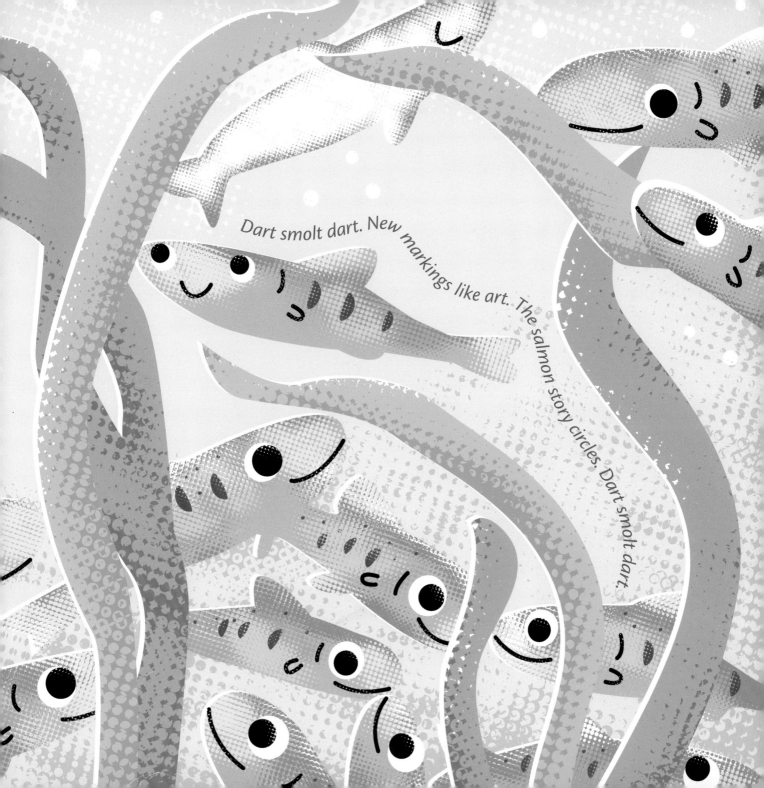

Dart smolt dart. New markings like art. The salmon story circles. Dart smolt dart.

Brave bright salmon, move far from shore.
Watch out for danger from whales, seals and more.
Brave bright salmon, glide through the sea.
A wish has come true. You are young, strong and free.

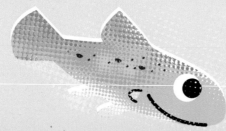

Glide salmon glide, through waters far and wide. The salmon story circles. Glide salmon glide.

Big strong salmon, travel afar.
Silver scales shine like a bright shooting star.
Big strong salmon, swim with the tide.
Eat fish and krill, journey side by side.

Swim salmon swim, a flash of silver skin. The salmon story circles. Swim salmon swim.

Full-grown salmon, a faint memory
calls out to you, "Return from the sea!"
Full-grown salmon, search on and on.
Find your home stream while you are still strong.

Search salmon search. Cedar, fir and birch. The salmon story circles. Search salmon search.

Brilliant red salmon, ending your trip.
Fly upstream past the bear's mighty grip.
Brilliant red salmon, leap through the air.
Rest will come soon. You are nearly there!

Leap salmon leap. Waterfalls so steep. The salmon story circles. Leap salmon leap.

See salmon spawn, from the forest trail.
We learn their story. A brave, selfless tale.

See salmon spawn, and share all as one.
The story that has ended has also begun.

Share children share, showing that you care. The salmon story circles. Share children share.

This story begins
unlike any other.

It starts at the end
for a father and mother.

They finish their journey
with one final wish...

...that the story
continues through
new baby fish.

Run salmon run, beneath the moon and sun. The salmon story circles...

...RUN SALMON RUN.

RUN SALMON RUN

Glossary

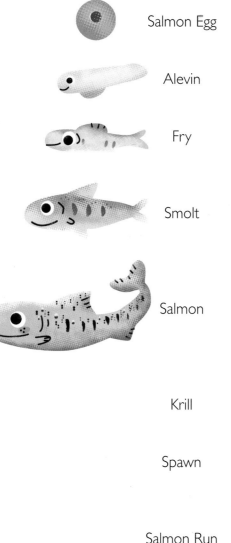

Salmon Egg — Adult salmon lay their **eggs** in gravel nests called redds. Baby salmon called alevin hatch from these eggs.

Alevin — *Alevin* are newly hatched trout or salmon. They carry the yolk sac from their egg with them; the yolk is their food.

Fry — Alevin grow into **fry**, and fry now swim to find food as their yolk sac has been absorbed. They also make a strong connection to their home stream; this is called "**imprinting**."

Smolt — Fry grow into **smolt**. Smolt go through a change where salt water is no longer absorbed into their bloodstream. This allows them to move from fresh water into salt water as they migrate to the ocean.

Salmon — A large fish that is born in streams but lives most of its life in the ocean. The Salmon is a "keystone" species in both water and land environments; this means that their presence can influence the survival or reproduction of other species.

Krill — Shrimp-like creatures that salmon and other marine animals feed on. **Krill** are found in all the world's oceans.

Spawn — When adult fish have finished growing they return to the rivers where they were born in order to **spawn**. Spawning is when adult fish pair up to make and lay eggs in a gravel nest, or redd.

Salmon Run — When salmon swim from the sea up into rivers to spawn.